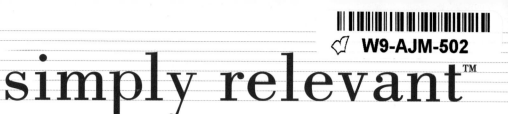

simply relevant™

{ SINGING IN THE RAIN }

Relational Bible Series for Women

Loveland, Colorado

Group resources really work!

This Group resource incorporates our R.E.A.L. approach to ministry. It reinforces a growing friendship with Jesus, encourages long-term learning, and results in life transformation, because it's:

Relational—Learner-to-learner interaction enhances learning and builds Christian friendships.

Experiential—What learners experience through discussion and action sticks with them up to 9 times longer than what they simply hear or read.

Applicable—The aim of Christian education is to equip learners to be both hearers and doers of God's Word.

Learner-based—Learners understand and retain more when the learning process takes into consideration how they learn best.

simply relevant™
Relational Bible Series for Women
{ SINGING IN THE RAIN }

Credits

Author: Amber Van Schooneveld
Executive Editor: Amy Nappa
Copy Editor: Ann Jahns
Chief Creative Officer: Joani Schultz
Cover Art Director: Paul Povolni
Cover Designer: Kate Elvin
Designers: Andrea Filer and Jean Bruns
Print Production Artist: Joyce Douglas
Production Manager: DeAnne Lear
Photographer (unless otherwise noted): Rodney Stewart
Photos on pages 9, 10, 16, 18, 19, 20, 25, 29, 30, 39, 40, 49, 50, 54, and 60 © istock.com

Unless otherwise indicated, all Scripture quotations are taken from the *Holy Bible,* New Living Translation, copyright © 1996, 2004. Used by permission of Tyndale House Publishers, Inc., Carol Stream, Illinois 60188. All rights reserved.

ISBN 978-0-7644-4141-7
10 9 8 7 6 5   19 18 17 16 15 14
Printed in the United States of America.

Contents

Introducing Simply Relevant | Singing in the Rain   5

Session 1: Our Reason for Joy   9
    Rejoicing in Our Relationship With God

Session 2: Joy in the Ups   19
    Remembering God in the Good Times

Session 3: Joy in the Downs   29
    Rejoicing That God's Promises Are True

Session 4: Joy in the Depths   39
    Rejoicing in God's Unfailing Love

Session 5: Joy in the Offering   49
    Rejoicing in Being Poured Out for Christ

Session 6: Joyfully Ever After   59
    Rejoicing Always With the Body of Christ

Welcome to *Simply Relevant: Singing in the Rain*! This is your totally relevant six-week Bible series that will help you develop relationships with other women as you grow in your joy in the Lord.

We all want to be joyful people, but it's not as easy as simply singing in the rain! This series will help you and your friends learn more about true joy and how we can experience it in all our circumstances—the ups *and* downs.

Each week, you'll learn what the Bible says true joy is (hint: It's not just happiness), how we can each experience it (it's *not* just putting on a happy face), and how we can be joyful even when we feel like we need an umbrella to shield us from all the bad things that seem to rain down in this world!

You can do this Bible series with five to 50 women—or even more! You want women to really grow in relationships with each other, so always get in small groups of four or five for discussion if you have a larger group. Women at any place in their faith journeys can feel right at home with this Bible series. The discussion questions can be understood and applied by women who don't know Jesus yet or women who are longtime friends with him. All the Bible passages are printed out for you, so those who aren't familiar with the Bible have the verses right in front of them.

So what will you be doing each week? Here's the structure of the sessions:

Note to the Hostess

Your hostess will be the woman facilitating your Bible series. She'll read the session through before the meeting, prepare for the activities, gather any supplies needed, and get the snacks ready. This box contains special tips just for the hostess, such as supplies to gather for the Experience, the atmosphere for the week, and ideas for snacks.

Mingling

Each week, you're going to start with snacks, mingling, and a short prayer. And this is key: Take time to share you how did with your previous week's commitment.

Experience

Each week you'll engage in an experience that will bring a new depth of meaning to the topic you'll explore. The experiences will get every woman involved and having fun. There might be a little bit of preparation or supplies needed, which the hostess will supply.

The Word

Each week, you'll read Scripture passages together and then, using questions from this guide, discuss what they mean. The questions are surprising, personal, and relevant to women today.

A Closer Look

These boxes provide a quick look at the Bible passages you'll be digging into each week. They'll help you develop a deeper understanding of the verses at hand while discussing their meaning in your lives. You can read them together during your session or on your own at home, but be sure to read them as they're important to the discussion.

Take Action

This is where women put faith into action. You'll all commit to apply what you've learned in a practical way during the coming week. You can write your own commitment or choose from the suggested commitments. Then next week, you'll check in with each other to see how you did.

Prayer

At the end of each session, you'll spend time in prayer together. You can ask for prayer requests and pray about the commitments you've made for the upcoming week. We've also given you a verse to read together to focus your minds for prayer.

Girlfriend Time

If you want some more hangout time together after your session is over, we've given you fun suggestions for easy activities to do together to reinforce the session's topic or to just relax. This is an optional bonus that will help you grow deeper in your friendships.

Still Thirsty?

If you want to explore the week's topic more, we've given you additional verses and reflection questions to read and consider in the coming week.

We pray that in the next six weeks, this experience will deepen your friendship with one another and, most of all, deepen your joy in the Lord as you serve and follow him.

—Group's Women's Ministry Team

Our Reason for Joy

Rejoicing in Our Relationship With God

Note to the Hostess:

This is the first week of your study on joy together, so make women comfortable and create an atmosphere of cheer. Greet your guests warmly—with the joy of the Lord! And chocolate chip cookies couldn't hurt either.

Read through the Experience section before your session, so you know how to prepare for this fun activity. The Scripture passage for this study presents the good news of salvation clearly. If you have guests who have never heard this message of salvation, you may want to take more time to discuss your experience of becoming a "friend of God."

Also, at the end of this session, ask women to bring some of their favorite photo albums, such as wedding albums or family vacation albums, for next week's session.

Get It...Got It?...Good.

- a warm greeting and smile for your guests
- chocolate chip cookies for extra cheer
- DVD or video of the movie *Singin' in the Rain* (and a TV and player so everyone can watch!)

Mingling

Enjoy the snacks the hostess has set out, and make sure you all know each other's names. Need a little help? Here's a conversation starter:

Hi, my name's [*your name*], and when I think about joy, the first word that pops into my head is _____.

Before starting, open your time by praying something like this:

> *God, thank you for bringing each individual woman here tonight. We thank you that you are the Author of joy and that we can find true joy in you. In Jesus' name, amen.*

Experience

(Note: The hostess will prepare and lead this experience this week.) Remember Gene Kelly and Debbie Reynolds from *Singin' in the Rain*? Ahhh…(If not, get thee to a Blockbuster or Netflix!) To start off your study, you'll watch Gene Kelly perform the title act of *Singin' in the Rain*. Check out the movie from the library or your favorite movie source (you can perhaps even find it online on YouTube), and cue it to Gene's singin' in the rain scene. This scene begins with Kelly saying goodbye to Reynolds at her front door and is approximately 1 hour and 8 minutes into the movie.

Show the clip to everyone, and then have women get into groups of four or five for discussion. Have groups use these questions and discuss them at their own pace:

Q: Whom do you think you're most often like in this clip—the man hustling by with an umbrella, trying to get out of the rain, or Gene, whose mood can't be dampened by rainy circumstances?

Q: Gene's happiness in this clip comes from his relationship with his cute companion, but where do you think real joy comes from?

the Word

Read Romans 5:8-11 together:

Romans 5:8-11*(italics added)*

But God showed his great love for us by sending Christ to die for us while we were still sinners. And since we have been made right in God's sight by the blood of Christ, he will certainly save us from God's condemnation. For since our friendship with God was restored by the death of his Son while we were still his enemies, we will certainly be saved through the life of his Son. So now *we can rejoice in our wonderful new relationship with God because our Lord Jesus Christ has made us friends of God.*

a closer look

Romans 5

Read this box before moving on to the Scripture Discussion Questions to take a deeper look at the verses for this session.

Romans 5:11 says that we can rejoice in our relationship with God. The Greek word that Paul uses in this verse for rejoice is *kauchaomai* (pronounced: kow-khah'-om-ahee), which means to glory or boast in something. We can *glory* in our wonderful relationship with God!

Of this verse, William MacDonald, in the *Believer's Bible Commentary*, says, "Before we were saved we found our joys elsewhere. Now we exult whenever we *remember* Him, and are sad only when we *forget* Him. What has produced this marvelous change, so that we can now be glad in God? It is the work of the Lord Jesus Christ."

scripture discussion questions

In groups of four or five, discuss these questions:

Q: Read MacDonald's quote in the A Closer Look section. In the past, where "elsewhere" have you found happiness that didn't come from your relationship with God?

Q: Have the "elsewheres" ever left you unsatisfied, or has the happiness been fleeting? Tell about it.

Q: This passage says that our relationship with God can be restored through the death of God's Son. In your own life, have you taken this step of becoming a "friend of God"? If not, we're glad you're here! If so, share your experience with the others.

Q: Think about these phrases from Romans 5:8-11: "great love," "restored," "saved," "rejoice," "wonderful new relationship," and "friends of God." What thoughts or emotions do they evoke in you?

Q: Over and over in the Bible, when the words *joy* or *rejoice* are used, it's in reference to the salvation we can find through Jesus Christ. Gene Kelly was right—it's not about our circumstances, but about a relationship! Have you ever experienced the kind of joy that makes you want to sing and dance in your relationship with God? If so, tell about it!

Take Action

Let's not just *talk* about the joy we can have through Jesus Christ, *let's experience it!* Write below how you're going to reflect on and "glory" in your relationship with God this week. If you're having a hard time thinking of something, choose one of the ideas below. Next week, you'll share with one another how you did.

this week

○ I'm going to rejoice in my wonderful new relationship in God by:

....

....

....

....

○ This week, I'm going to learn more about how I can begin a friendship with God by talking this week's passage over with a good friend.

○ This week, I'm going to read the verses in the Still Thirsty? section and meditate on the questions.

○ This week, I'm going to keep track of where I'm trying to find my joy or happiness. When it's in the wrong place, I'll pray for God to help me find my joy in him.

Prayer

End your time together in prayer to your Father. Read Psalm 13:5 together.

> *But I trust in your unfailing love. I will rejoice because you have rescued me.*

Rejoice! God has rescued us. Thank God for the salvation and relationship you can have with him through Jesus Christ. Ask him to help you find real joy in him.

Girlfriend Time

If you want to spend more time together with your friends, watch the rest of *Singin' in the Rain*. Nothing like a good, old-fashioned romance to bond with friends.

Still Thirsty?

If you're still thirsty to know more about finding joy in God's salvation, check out these Scriptures:

Isaiah 25:9

"In that day the people will proclaim, 'This is our God! We trusted in him, and he saved us! This is the Lord, in whom we trusted. Let us rejoice in the salvation he brings!' "

Q: How do you think trusting in God and joy are related to each other?

Luke 10:20

"But don't rejoice because evil spirits obey you; rejoice because your names are registered in heaven."

Q: Jesus told his disciples to rejoice not in the spiritual power they had found, but in their salvation. Can you find any parallel in your own life?

Psalm 13:5

"But I trust in your unfailing love. I will rejoice because you have rescued me."

Q: In what way has God rescued you? Spend some time thinking about the ways, and then spend some time rejoicing in them!

Romans 12:12

"Rejoice in our confident hope. Be patient in trouble, and keep on praying."

Q: How confident would you say your own hope is?

Joy in the Ups

Remembering God in the Good Times

Note to the Hostess:

This week, you're going to be discussing how we can remember God and rejoice in him even in the good times—when everything seems to be hunky-dory. God promised to bring the Israelites to a land of milk and honey. But once they were in that land of milk

and honey, the Israelites had a tendency to forget God.

Serve a snack of milk and biscuits with honey, to symbolize this place of comfort. (For an easier snack, you could also serve honey graham crackers.) You'll refer back to the snack during the Scripture Discussion Questions.

For the Experience this week, women will be looking through their old photo albums, so be sure to ask women to bring some of their favorite photo albums before this session.

Get It...Got It?...Good.

- milk
- biscuits with honey (or honey graham crackers)
- photo albums
- a heart that remembers God

Mingling

Enjoy the snacks the hostess has set out, and talk about what you did last week to experience the joy of a relationship with God.

Before starting, open your time by praying something like this:

God, thank you that we can gather here to rejoice together in you. We pray that tonight you would help us to always have you—not our circumstances—as the center of our joy. In Jesus' name, amen.

Experience

Get in pairs or small groups of four or five, and have fun looking through some of your favorite photos that remind you of the good times God has given you. The photos might be from a favorite family vacation or a wedding day or a baby's birth.

While you look through the photos, discuss the following with your partner or small group.

Q: Tell about one of your happiest or most joyful memories. (A wedding? A child's first steps? A vacation?)

Take about 15 minutes for looking at photos and sharing stories. Be sure everyone in your group has a chance to share! Once the time is up, get back together to read the Word together.

the Word

Read Deuteronomy 8:10-14 and 17-18 together:

Deuteronomy 8:10-14, 17-18

When you have eaten your fill, be sure to praise the Lord your God for the good land he has given you. But that is the time to be careful! Beware that in your plenty you do not forget the Lord your God and disobey his commands, regulations, and decrees that I am giving you today. For when you have become full and prosperous and have built fine homes to live in, and when your flocks and herds have become very large and your silver and gold have multiplied along with everything else, be careful! Do not become proud at that time and forget the Lord your God, who rescued you from slavery in the land of Egypt…

He did all this so you would never say to yourself, "I have achieved this wealth with my own strength and energy." Remember the Lord your God. He is the one who gives you power to be successful, in order to fulfill the covenant he confirmed to your ancestors with an oath.

a closer look

1 Thessalonians

*Read this box before moving on to the Scripture Discussion Questions
to take a deeper look at the verses for this session.*

These verses warn about what continually happened to the Israelites:
Prosperity and physical comfort led to forgetfulness of God. When
we're comfortable, we often find our happiness or contentment in our
circumstances, rather than finding our joy in God.

But as Billy Graham points out in *The Holy Spirit*, the verses in the New
Testament about joy repeatedly point to a *spiritual* source of joy, such as
the "joy of the Holy Spirit" in I Thessalonians 1:6. In the Old Testament, the
verses about joy also point to God as the source of joy in repeated phrases
such as "the joy of the Lord" in Nehemiah 8:10. Our source of joy isn't our
happy circumstances; *God* is the source of joy.

scripture discussion questions

In groups of four or five, discuss these questions:

Q: God promised to bring the Israelites to a land of milk and honey, but once they
got to the comfortable place, they tended to forget all about him. Many of us are
in situations of comfort—we literally can have milk and honey anytime we want it.
When you are in a comfortable spot in life, do you tend to forget about God?
Tell about a time this was the case.

Q: This Scripture passage talks about the things that made the Israelites forgetful of finding their joy and hope in God—their fine homes, flocks, herds, silver, and gold. You might not have any flocks or hordes of silver, but what is your equivalent of this today? What things in your life tend to make you forget God?

Q: There's nothing wrong with honey or homes or herds—God wanted these things for the Israelites. The question is, How do we remember to rejoice in God and not in our possessions or good circumstances?

Q: When times are good, what are some ways you can consciously remember to find your joy in God and praise him?

Q: As you read in the A Closer Look section, the verses in the Bible that talk about joy continuously point to God as the source of joy. But when times were good, the Israelites tended to think *they* were the ones who had achieved all the goodness in their lives, as it says in verse 17. When have you struggled with thinking that the good things in your life came about because of your own strength and energy, the way the Israelites did?

Q: Rather than having the "ups" in life be a cause of forgetfulness, how can you actively use the good gifts and good times God has given you to bring praise to him?

Take Action

Let's not just *talk* about having God as the source of our joy, *let's do it!* Write below how you're going to remember God in the good times this week. If you're having a hard time thinking of something, choose one of the ideas below. Next week, you'll share with one another how you did.

this week

I'm going to remember God this week by:

This week, I'm going to remember to praise God and rejoice in him before each meal, to remember that all my good gifts come from him.

This week, I'm going to read the verses in the Still Thirsty? section and meditate on the questions.

This week, I'm going to spend some alone time with God praying about whether or not I have forgotten him in the good times.

Prayer

End your time together in prayer to your Father. Read James 1:17 together.

> "Whatever is good and perfect comes down to us from God our Father, who created all the lights in the heavens. He never changes or casts a shifting shadow."

Thank God for all his good gifts in your life. Ask that he would help you to praise him and rejoice in him every day, even when things seem to be going just fine. Thank him for his faithfulness to you.

Girlfriend Time

If you want to spend more time together with your friends, there's nothing more bonding than looking at old family photo albums together! Spend some more time looking through your photo albums together to remember the good times God has given you.

Still Thirsty?

If you're still thirsty to know more about rejoicing in the good times, check out these Scriptures:

Ecclesiastes 12:1-3

"Don't let the excitement of youth cause you to forget your Creator. Honor him in your youth before you grow old and say, 'Life is not pleasant anymore.' Remember him before the light of the sun, moon, and stars is dim to your old eyes, and rain clouds continually darken your sky. Remember him before your legs—the guards of your house—start to tremble; and before your shoulders—the strong men—stoop. Remember him before your teeth—your few remaining servants—stop grinding; and before your eyes—the women looking through the windows—see dimly."

Q: Why do you think it's important to remember God in our youth—when we're still strong and healthy?

1 Chronicles 16:8-10

"Give thanks to the Lord and proclaim his greatness. Let the whole world know what he has done. Sing to him; yes, sing his praises. Tell everyone about his wonderful deeds. Exult in his holy name; rejoice, you who worship the Lord."

Q: David exhorts us to rejoice in God and tell everyone about the good things he has done for us. Spend some time reflecting about God's wonderful deeds for you.

James 1:17

"Whatever is good and perfect comes down to us from God our Father, who created all the lights in the heavens. He never changes or casts a shifting shadow."

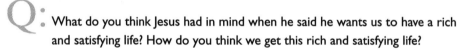 Do you believe that everything that is good in your life has come from God? Spend some time thinking about all the good things, and then thank God for each one.

John 10:10

"The thief's purpose is to steal and kill and destroy. My purpose is to give them a rich and satisfying life."

Q: What do you think Jesus had in mind when he said he wants us to have a rich and satisfying life? How do you think we get this rich and satisfying life?

Notes

Joy in the Downs

Rejoicing That God's Promises Are True

Note to the Hostess:

This week may be a hard one. You'll be discussing how we can be joyful even when life is hard. The women in your group may be experiencing some truly difficult things, such as cancer, depression, unemployment, infertility, and so on. So as you ask questions, be sensitive to where your friends are at and what they're comfortable sharing.

Serve a simple snack of fruit and tea. If you want to have a theme, you could serve the foods mentioned in this week's passage: figs, grapes, and olives, and draw this into your discussion about when life *doesn't* give you grapes and olives.

Read through the Experience this week, to learn how to prepare for this simple activity. If you think you'll want to spend more time together after the session, read through the Girlfriend Time before your session.

Get It...Got It?...Good.

- a simple snack like fruit and tea; or figs, grapes, and olives
- a listening ear
- (optional) scrapbooking supplies for Girlfriend Time

Mingling

Enjoy the snacks the hostess has set out, and talk about what you did last week to rejoice in day-to-day life.

Before starting, open your time by praying something like this:

Dear Lord, we praise you that you are God all the time—in the ups and in the downs of life. We know that we can trust you and your promises. Help us to trust in you, even in the valleys of life. In Jesus' name, amen.

Experience

Gather into groups of four or five. Have someone read aloud the Word for this week, Habakkuk 3:17-19. The things the prophet wrote about in this passage were crucial in his time. People were dependent on their crops and herds for their livelihood. But what Habakkuk mentions may not necessarily reflect our own experience.

Think through the passage, and brainstorm in your small groups about what our modern-day equivalents are to a fig tree not blossoming or a grapevine not producing, a field being empty, and the flocks dying in the fields. Maybe it's, "Even though I didn't get this job," or "even though my mom has cancer," or "even though my car is broken down."

Use the space on the next page to write your own version. (You can even write your own version of the last line…"He makes me as sturdy as the SUV, able to climb the icy hill…")

Take turns reading what you've written to the group, if you're comfortable. Once you are finished, read the A Closer Look section together.

the Word

Read Habakkuk 3:17-19 together:

Habakkuk 3:17-19

Even though the fig trees have no blossoms,

and there are no grapes on the vines;

even though the olive crop fails,

and the fields lie empty and barren;

even though the flocks die in the fields,

and the cattle barns are empty,

yet I will rejoice in the Lord!

I will be joyful in the God of my salvation!

The Sovereign Lord is my strength!

He makes me as surefooted as a deer,

able to tread upon the heights.

a closer look

Habakkuk 3

*Read this box before moving on to the Scripture Discussion Questions
to take a deeper look at the verses for this session.*

In Habakkuk 3, the prophet is still able to rejoice in God, even though, looking around him, he sees no reason to. The crops are dead, and so are the cattle. But in the context of this passage, it is clear that Habakkuk still hopes and believes that God will come and fulfill his promises to his people. In chapter 3, he remembers how God has delivered Israel in the past. Verse 16, which precedes this passage says, "I will wait quietly for the coming day when disaster will strike the people who invade us." Habakkuk takes heart because even though things are bleak, he knows God will fulfill his promises in time and that God *is* a God of salvation. But he doesn't just "wait quietly." The phrase in Habakkuk 3:18 literally means, "I will *jump for joy* in the Lord!" Our joy, even in times of despair, can lead us to *leap* for joy!

scripture discussion questions

In groups of four or five, discuss these questions:

Q: When have you been in a situation like Habakkuk describes, when outwardly everything is going wrong? Were you able to "yet" rejoice in the Lord?

Q: Habakkuk 3:2 says, "In this time of our deep need, help us again as you did in years gone by." Before this passage, Habakkuk remembers what God has done in the past for the Israelites. How do you think remembering how God has helped you in the past allows you to rejoice in God today?

Q: Habakkuk says he "waits quietly" for the day God fulfills his promises. How are you waiting? Quietly? Or another way? Tell about it.

Q: What promises has God given you that you can put your trust in, even when you're in a time of waiting or suffering?

Q: The literal translation of *joy* in this passage is *"jump* for joy". When have you experienced that kind of joy? How are you most likely to express joy?

Take Action

Let's not just *talk* about rejoicing in God's promises, *let's do it!* Write below how you're going to rejoice in God's promises this week. If you're having a hard time thinking of something, choose one of the ideas below. Next week, you'll share with one another how you did.

this week

○ I'm going to rejoice this week by:

....

....

....

....

○ This week, I'm going to write down all of the ways God has helped me in the past.

○ This week, I'm going to write down the promises God has given me in the Scriptures to remember in troubled times.

○ This week, I'm going to read the verses in the Still Thirsty? section and meditate on the questions.

Prayer

End your time together in prayer to your Father. Read Psalm 30:5 together.

> "Weeping may last through the night, but joy comes with the morning."

Pray to God, acknowledging that some of us may be in a phase of weeping and the night. But praise him that we know that in these dark times we can hold strong to his promises, knowing that his morning of salvation will dawn. Ask him to help us seek him always in these times and look to him for our joy and our strength.

Girlfriend Time

If you want to spend more time hanging out together, you can create scrapbook pages for Habakkuk 3:17-19 using the personal versions you wrote in the Experience. As you scrapbook, talk more about times you've been able to experience joy in the Lord, even when the proverbial fig tree didn't blossom.

Still Thirsty?

If you're still thirsty to know more about rejoicing in God in the hard times, check out these Scriptures:

Joel 2:23-26

"Rejoice, you people of Jerusalem! Rejoice in the Lord your God! For the rain he sends demonstrates his faithfulness. Once more the autumn rains will come, as well as the rains of spring. The threshing floors will again be piled high with grain, and the presses will overflow with new wine and olive oil.

"The Lord says, 'I will give you back what you lost to the swarming locusts, the hopping locusts, the stripping locusts, and the cutting locusts. It was I who sent this great destroying army against you.

" 'Once again you will have all the food you want, and you will praise the Lord your God, who does these miracles for you. Never again will my people be disgraced.' "

Q: God promised to repay the Israelites for the years of desolation, the years of locusts, with years of plenty. What do you think you can infer about the character of God from this?

Psalm 139:16

"You saw me before I was born. Every day of my life was recorded in your book. Every moment was laid out before a single day had passed."

Q: How does it comfort you to know that God knows your days and has laid them out before you?

1 Peter 1:6

"So be truly glad. There is wonderful joy ahead, even though you have to endure many trials for a little while."

Q: What do you think Peter meant by "wonderful joy ahead"?

1 Chronicles 16:10-11

"Exult in his holy name; rejoice, you who worship the Lord. Search for the Lord and for his strength; continually seek him."

Q: How do you think these two lines are related? How does searching for the Lord continually help you to worship him?

Joy in the Depths

Rejoicing in God's Unfailing Love

Note to the Hostess:

This week you'll focus in more on rejoicing even when we are in the depths of a dark valley. Like last week, be sensitive to what your friends are going through and to the Holy Spirit's leading. If you feel the Holy Spirit leading you to stop and pray for a particular woman, be responsive to his call!

Serve a comfy, simple snack to make women feel welcome, such as milk and cookies. You don't need to gather any supplies for the Experience this week; just read through the section before your session to prepare.

Get It...Got It?...Good.

- ⦿ a comfy snack, such as milk and cookies
- ⦿ a heart of compassion

Mingling

Enjoy the snacks the hostess has set out, and talk about what you did last week to rejoice in God.

Before starting, open your time by praying something like this:

God, we thank you that you love each one of us here, and that we can trust you even when we are in a deep valley of life. We pray that you would help us learn to rejoice in your unfailing love. In Jesus' name, amen.

Experience

Note: The hostess will prepare the Experience before your session.

Before your session, ask a trusted friend if she would share her testimony of a dark time that God has brought her through (or share your own story). It might be a time in which she felt much like David in Psalm 31 and cried out in anguish to God. Have the woman share how she was able to get through that time and keep her joy in the Lord. Have her also share her perspective on it now and what she learned through that time.

After she has shared, you can ask if any other women would like to share a similar experience, or transition into reading the Word together. Allow time for sharing.

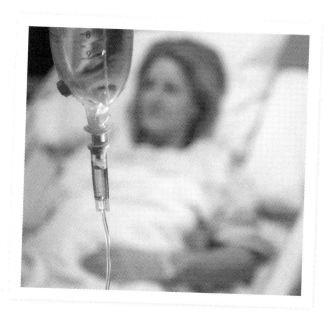

the Word

Read Psalm 31:7-10 and 14 together:

Psalm 31:7-10, 14

I will be glad and rejoice in your unfailing love, for you have seen my troubles, and you care about the anguish of my soul. You have not handed me over to my enemies but have set me in a safe place.

Have mercy on me, Lord, for I am in distress. Tears blur my eyes. My body and soul are withering away. I am dying from grief; my years are shortened by sadness. Sin has drained my strength; I am wasting away from within...

But I am trusting you, O Lord, saying, "You are my God!"

a closer look

Read this box before moving on to the Scripture Discussion Questions to take a deeper look at the verses for this session.

In Psalm 31, David was in real anguish. People were literally hunting him down to kill him. His eyes were blurred from crying; his soul was withering. David was in torment. And yet in verse 7, he could still rejoice and be glad in God's unfailing love.

He gives two reasons: because God *saw* his troubles, and because God *cared* about the anguish of David's soul. The first time God was called "the God who sees," or "El Roi," was by a woman in anguish, Hagar. Just as God saw Hagar crying in the desert in her despair (Genesis 16:13), God saw David in his distress, and God sees you.

scripture discussion questions

In groups of four or five, discuss these questions:

Q: How does it make you feel to know that God sees you, even in the time of your greatest distress?

Q: When you're in a time of suffering, is it hard for you to believe in your heart of hearts that God cares about the anguish of your soul? Discuss your thoughts.

Q: Hebrews 4:15 says, "This High Priest of ours [Jesus] understands our weaknesses, for he faced all of the same testings we do."

Not only do we have a God who sees us in our suffering, we have a God who knows and has experienced the deepest suffering. How does this comfort you?

Q: In Psalm 31, David goes back and forth between crying out in anguish in one breath, and praising and rejoicing in God in another. Relate this to your own experiences. Where do you most often find yourself on the spectrum?

Q: When we are going through times of suffering, it doesn't always feel like God loves us. How can you still rejoice in God's "unfailing love" when your situation doesn't make you feel loved?

Take Action

Let's not just *talk* about rejoicing in God's unfailing love, *let's do it*! Write below how you're going to rejoice in God's unfailing love this week. If you're having a hard time thinking of something, choose one of the ideas below. Next week, you'll share with one another how you did.

this week

○ I'm going to rejoice this week by:

○ This week, I'll pray through all of Psalm 31, asking that God will help me rejoice in him, even when my soul is in anguish.

○ This week, I'm going to spend some alone time with God praying or journaling about whether or not I truly believe that he sees me, he cares about my anguish, and he loves me.

○ This week, I'm going to read the verses in the Still Thirsty? section and meditate on the questions.

Prayer

End your time together in prayer to your Father.
Read Psalm 23:4 together.

> "Even when I walk through the darkest valley, I will not be afraid, for you are close beside me."

Praise God that he is a God who sees us in our suffering, and a God who walks close beside us even in the darkest of valleys. Ask that he would help us to trust in him and rejoice in his unfailing love, even when we are in anguish.

Girlfriend Time

If you want to spend more time together with your friends, consider having a time of prayer together. You may have uncovered some areas in your lives this week that need God's healing. Take time to hear one another's needs for God's unfailing love to heal them, and then spend time praying for it.

Still Thirsty?

If you're still thirsty to know more about rejoicing even in the depths, check out these Scriptures:

Psalm 23:4, 6

"Even when I walk through the darkest valley, I will not be afraid, for you are close beside me…Surely your goodness and unfailing love will pursue me all the days of my life, and I will live in the house of the Lord forever."

Q: Meditate on the image of God walking close beside you in a dark valley. Then meditate on the image of God's unfailing love *pursuing* you.

Lamentations 3:31-33

"For no one is abandoned by the Lord forever. Though he brings grief, he also shows compassion because of the greatness of his unfailing love. For he does not enjoy hurting people or causing them sorrow."

Q: If you have felt abandoned by God, did it make you question his unfailing love? Do you think you have dealt with this?

Job 13:15

"Though he slay me, yet will I hope in him." (New International Version)

Q: Consider your level of trust in God. Do you have the kind of trust in God that even if he killed you, you would put your hope in him? Write your thoughts about this.

Psalm 119:76-77

"Now let your unfailing love comfort me, just as you promised me, your servant. Surround me with your tender mercies so I may live, for your instructions are my delight."

Q: How often do you turn to God's love for comfort in times of trial? How often do you turn to something else?

Notes

Joy in the Offering

Rejoicing in Being Poured Out for Christ

Note to the Hostess:

This week you'll discuss rejoicing in God as you pour yourselves out to him and suffer for him. Serve an easy snack, such as cheese and crackers.

This week, you'll do the Experience *after* the Scripture Discussion Questions. Read through the Experience before your session, so you know how to prepare. Also, read through next week's session, so you know how to prepare for that.

Get It...Got It?...Good.

- an easy snack, like cheese and crackers
- one glass of water per woman
- a sink or a large bowl
- a heart given over to God

Mingling

Enjoy the snacks the hostess has set out, and talk about what you did last week to find joy in God.

Before starting, open your time by praying something like this:

> Dear God, we praise you that we have the privilege of serving you. We pray that you would help us to find joy in giving our lives to you. In Jesus' name, amen.

the Word

Read Philippians 2:17-18 and Matthew 10:38-39 together:

Philippians 2:17-18

But I will rejoice even if I lose my life, pouring it out like a liquid offering to God, just like your faithful service is an offering to God. And I want all of you to share that joy. Yes, you should rejoice, and I will share your joy.

Matthew 10:38-39

If you refuse to take up your cross and follow me, you are not worthy of being mine. If you cling to your life, you will lose it; but if you give up your life for me, you will find it.

a closer look

Read this box before moving on to the Scripture Discussion Questions to take a deeper look at the verses for this session.

Throughout the New Testament, Paul says that he rejoices *because of* trials and sufferings, not despite them. In Philippians 2:17, Paul likens his own trials—imprisonment and potential death—to a sacrifice, or liquid offering, to God. The church he was writing to in Philippi was in an extremely hostile pagan environment where Christians suffered harsh persecution. Many of us today might not be able to relate to this, if we live in places where our freedom and very life aren't at risk for our Christian faith.

However, just as Paul referred to his own imprisonment as an offering, he calls the "faithful service" of the church at Philippi an offering to God. Although we may not face martyrdom, we do pour out our lives in our *faith* and in our *service* as our sacrifice to God. As Bible commentator John MacArthur, Jr. put it, "Sacrificial service to the Lord is in itself a privilege and a cause for rejoicing."

scripture discussion questions

In groups of four or five, discuss these questions:

Q: Although in some parts of the world, Christians still face severe persecution, many of us don't face the same kind of persecution the first-century church did. In what ways *have* you suffered because of your faith in Christ? Have you rejoiced *because* you suffered?

Q: Paul calls the Philippians' "faithful service" their sacrifice to God. Some have joked that the problem with a living sacrifice is that it keeps crawling off the altar. How have you offered your life as a sacrifice for God to use? When have you had problems crawling off the altar?

Q: Even if you don't face persecution, in what ways can you daily offer yourself as an offering to God?

Q: Jesus makes the counterintuitive statement that "if you cling to your life, you will lose it; but if you give up your life for me, you will find it." How, when you have given up your life for Christ, have you truly found life?

Q: How, in giving up your life for Christ as an offering to him, have you found true joy?

Experience

Note: The hostess will prepare the Experience before your session and will lead it.

Give a glass of water to each woman, and have women gather around a sink or a large bowl (large enough to hold the water from all the women's glasses). Then ask this question:

Q: Think of the water in this glass as your life. Are there any areas of your life that you are holding back from God?

Women can discuss this question aloud or silently contemplate it for a moment. Then have women simultaneously and slowly pour their glasses out as a symbol of offering themselves to God, as you pray something like this (or as they each pray silently to themselves):

> *Dear Lord, we offer ourselves to you as liquid offerings. We want to offer you all of us—our bodies, our minds, our daily life, our work, our family—as we serve you. We thank you that we have the privilege and joy of serving you and sacrificing ourselves for you. We pray that you would help us each day to offer ourselves anew to you.*

Allow a few minutes of silence after women have emptied their glasses so they can continue to reflect on this commitment. If women are comfortable sharing, allow them to tell about what they "poured" out as an offering to God.

Take Action

Let's not just *talk* about rejoicing in being poured out for Christ, *let's do it*! Write below how you're going to find joy in serving Christ this week. If you're having a hard time thinking of something, choose one of the ideas below. Next week, you'll share with one another how you did.

this week

○ I'm going to find joy in serving Christ this week by:

....

....

....

....

○ This week, I'll meditate on Christ's words in Matthew 10 and consider if I truly have picked up my cross to follow him.

○ This week, I'll spend time talking to God about whether I am truly pouring myself out for him or keeping back part of myself.

○ This week, I'm going to read the verses in the Still Thirsty? section and meditate on the questions.

Prayer

End your time together in prayer to your Father.
Read 1 Peter 4:13 together.

> For these trials make you partners with Christ in his suffering, so that you will have the wonderful joy of seeing his glory when it is revealed to all the world.

Praise God that you can be partners with Christ in his suffering. Offer yourselves up to him as living sacrifices to be used by him. Pray that he would help you to know the wonderful joy of serving Christ.

Girlfriend Time

If you want more hang time with the girls, share some gab time talking about your walk thus far with God. What ups and downs have you had? Have you had times of close walking with God, placing yourself on his altar each day, and times of wandering? Spend time sharing your testimonies and talking about where you think you are right now.

Still Thirsty?

If you're still thirsty to rejoice as we are poured out for Christ, check out these Scriptures:

1 Peter 4:12-13

"Dear friends, don't be surprised at the fiery trials you are going through, as if something strange were happening to you. Instead, be very glad—for these trials make you partners with Christ in his suffering, so that you will have the wonderful joy of seeing his glory when it is revealed to all the world."

Q: Have you ever considered yourself a "partner" with Christ? In what way do you think this is true as you serve him?

James 1:2-4

"Dear brothers and sisters, when troubles come your way, consider it an opportunity for great joy. For you know that when your faith is tested, your endurance has a chance to grow. So let it grow, for when your endurance is fully developed, you will be perfect and complete, needing nothing."

Q: Think back. Can you remember a time of trial that resulted in endurance? How did this trial end up bringing you joy?

Romans 5:3-4

"We can rejoice, too, when we run into problems and trials, for we know that they help us develop endurance. And endurance develops strength of character, and character strengthens our confident hope of salvation."

Q: How has a trial you have gone through strengthened your confident hope in salvation?

Luke 6:22-23

"What blessings await you when people hate you and exclude you and mock you and curse you as evil because you follow the Son of Man. When that happens, be happy! Yes, leap for joy! For a great reward awaits you in heaven. And remember, their ancestors treated the ancient prophets that same way."

Q: Have you ever been hated, excluded, or mocked for Jesus? If not, why do you think that is? Consider how you might pray for those who are currently being mistreated, often severely, for their faith in God.

Joyfully Ever After

Rejoicing Always With the Body of Christ

Note to the Hostess:

Your last week together—it's time to rejoice and celebrate! You'll be focusing on how we can rejoice together as the body of Christ, so use this as an opportunity to celebrate.

Ask friends to each bring a dish and celebrate a meal together. You don't need to gather anything to prepare for the Experience this week, but if you celebrate a meal together remember to plan for it the previous week.

Get It...Got It?...Good.

- a potluck meal to celebrate
- a spirit of joy

Mingling

Before you begin your meal, talk about what you did last week to find your joy in serving God.

Before starting, open your time by praying something like this:

Dear Lord, we thank you that we can rejoice every day in you, no matter our circumstances. We thank you that you've given us your family so we can experience your joy together. In Jesus' name, amen.

Experience

For your Experience this week, enjoy your meal together. While you eat, have women tell one another what their personal fairy tale was when they were younger—their "happily ever after." It might be that they hoped to be a mom with four children and a white picket fence and a Prince Charming, or maybe they dreamt of being a missionary in a far-

off place having adventures, or maybe they dreamt of being a lawyer and handling high-stakes cases.

After each woman has told her fairy tale, have women answer this question:

Q: Now that you're older, what do you think it means to live happily ever after, or "joyfully ever after"?

the Word

Have different woman read the passages below out loud:

1 Thessalonians 5:16

Always be joyful.

Philippians 4:4

Always be full of joy in the Lord. I say it again—rejoice!

Galatians 5:22-23

But the Holy Spirit produces this kind of fruit in our lives: love, joy, peace, patience, kindness, goodness, faithfulness, gentleness, and self-control.

Philemon 1:7

Your love has given me much joy and comfort, my brother, for your kindness has often refreshed the hearts of God's people.

1 Thessalonians 2:19-20

After all, what gives us hope and joy, and what will be our proud reward and crown as we stand before our Lord Jesus when he returns? It is you! Yes, you are our pride and joy.

a closer look

*Read this box before moving on to the Scripture Discussion Questions
to take a deeper look at the verses for this session.*

We've learned that joy comes not from our circumstances, but from our relationship with God. And we don't experience that joy alone. God hasn't called us to simply be ascetics living alone on a hillside, seeing no face but his. God created us to rejoice together as his family of believers and experience his joy together. As in the verses in Philemon and 1 Thessalonians, Paul often wrote that the saints were his joy—he found joy in their salvation, in praying for them, and in seeing them grow to become like Christ. The world will see our joy in Christ as they see us in relationship with one another, rejoicing together in what God has done for us.

scripture discussion questions

In groups of four or five, discuss these questions:

Q: The verses we read in 1 Thessalonians 5 and Philippians command us to be joyful always, as if it's a choice we make...But how do you practically choose to become joyful? What does this mean *in day-to-day life* for you?

Q: In Galatians 5, it says that the fruit the Holy Spirit creates in us is joy. How do you practically ensure that you are living through the Holy Spirit?

Q: Paul was joyful, in part, because of the saints around him. List and share some ways in which your family of Christians makes you joyful and helps you to rejoice in God.

Q: Have you ever considered your joy coming from doing life with the body of Christ or the church? Do you think someone looking at your life from the outside would see this reflected in the way you live your life?

Q: Brainstorm some ways you can live as the first-century church did, rejoicing together in God.

Take Action

Let's not just *talk* about rejoicing together, *let's do it*! Write below how you're going to experience God's joy together after this study. If you're having a hard time thinking of something, choose one of the ideas below.

this week

○ I'm going to rejoice by:

....

....

....

....

○ I'm going to plan a celebration with other believers so that we can rejoice together in what God is doing in our lives.

○ I'm going to spend more time with the body of believers, rather than try to develop my relationship with God alone.

○ This week, I'm going to read the verses in the Still Thirsty? section and meditate on the questions.

Prayer

End your time together in prayer to your Father.
Read Psalm 118:24 together.

> "This is the day the Lord has made. We will rejoice and be glad in it."

Thank God for the time you've spent together these six weeks. Spend some time rejoicing in God in prayer and thanking God for the joy he has for you each day of your lives in him.

Girlfriend Time

If you want to spend more time with your friends, spend some time celebrating together! You could just enjoy some simple hangout time or build up your relationships with one another by going around the room and sharing what you appreciate about each woman.

Still Thirsty?

If you're still thirsty to know more about rejoicing in God and in the body of Christ, check out these Scriptures:

1 Thessalonians 3:9

"How we thank God for you! Because of you we have great joy as we enter God's presence."

Q: Is there anyone you've been able to influence for Christ who brings you great joy? How can you let that person know the joy he or she brings to you?

3 John 1:4

"I could have no greater joy than to hear that my children are following the truth."

Q: What brings you the greatest joy? How is this verse true or untrue for your own life?

Philippians 1:4

"Whenever I pray, I make my requests for all of you with joy."

Q: Do you pray with joy for other Christians? What might that look like or sound like if you began?

Romans 15:13

"I pray that God, the source of hope, will fill you completely with joy and peace because you trust in him. Then you will overflow with confident hope through the power of the Holy Spirit."

Q: What does it mean to you to overflow with hope because of the joy God has given you? How is this evident in your own life?